To Jill,
the Chewbacca Mom
(that was) —
YOU JUST WAIT

Happy reading
+ writing!

YOU JUST WAIT

A POETRY FRIDAY POWER BOOK

12 POWERPLAY PREWRITING ACTIVITIES
+12 POEMS FROM THE POETRY FRIDAY ANTHOLOGY FOR MIDDLE SCHOOL
+24 NEW POEMS TO JOIN THEM TOGETHER
+12 POWER2YOU WRITING PROMPTS
+12 RESOURCE LISTS FOR WRITERS

BY
SYLVIA VARDELL AND JANET WONG

∞

THIS BOOK IS DEDICATED
TO LEE BENNETT HOPKINS
WITH GRATITUDE
FOR YOUR GROUNDBREAKING WORK
IN CREATING POETRY ANTHOLOGIES

&

WITH SPECIAL THANKS TO OUR ADVANCE READERS
DAVID BOWLES, MARGARITA ENGLE, CAROL JAGO,
ELAINE MAGLIARO, PAT MORA, LINDA SUE PARK,
AND OUR FRIENDS AT THE 2016 MILLERSVILLE UNIVERSITY POETRY INSTITUTE
FOR YOUR INSIGHTS & SUPPORT

∞

Pomelo Books
4580 Province Line Road
Princeton, NJ 08540
PomeloBooks.com
info@PomeloBooks.com

Copyright ©2016 Pomelo Books. All rights reserved.
Illustrations by Topform84 at iStockPhoto.com
Poems copyright ©2013 and ©2016 by the individual poets; refer to credits. All rights reserved. The Poetry Friday Anthology® is a registered trademark of Pomelo Books.
Library of Congress Cataloging-in-Publication Data is available.
ISBN 978-1-937057-62-6

Please visit us:
POMELOBOOKS.COM

TABLE OF CONTENTS

Here is a list of the "Poetry Friday" poems that anchor each cluster or PowerPack of activities, response poems, mentor texts, and writing prompts, along with other components that make this book interactive.

A POETRY FRIDAY POWER BOOK

Why is this a "Poetry Friday Power Book"? Because we believe in the power of poetry to express our deepest feelings and most powerful experiences. Plus, we want you to discover the power of poetry in your own thinking and writing with the PowerPlay pre-writing and Power2You writing prompts that pull you into poetry and inspire you to get your own ideas on paper—creatively, whimsically, powerfully, and immediately—right now in this book.

And why "Poetry Friday"? Because we found our inspiration for this book in twelve of the 700+ poems from *The Poetry Friday Anthology*® series—specifically, twelve poems written by a variety of award-winning poets and previously published in *The Poetry Friday Anthology for Middle School*. We used these Poetry Friday poems as the starting point for a story about identity, sports, dreams, and frustrations—connecting them with 24 new poems.

This is a fanfiction model of what you can do when you read, gather, and collect your favorite poems from a variety of sources. Even though the poems may be by many different poets, on many different topics, from many different books, magazines, or online sources, YOU are the one who sees the connection between them, hears the voices in your mind, and can write your own poems to weave those poems together to create a story only you can tell.

This book offers you several choices for reading, thinking, writing, and responding. Overall, it's a story in poems, but all of this is also organized in PowerPack groups that help you get a "behind the scenes" look at how poems work and how poets write and think. In each of these PowerPack groups, you'll find five things:
- PowerPlay activity
- Outside poem (from another poetry book)
- Response poem
- Mentor text
- Power2You poem writing prompt

Have fun reading and thinking about poetry and learning about how poetry uses just a few words, but says so much. Ready? Let's "power up" and get started!

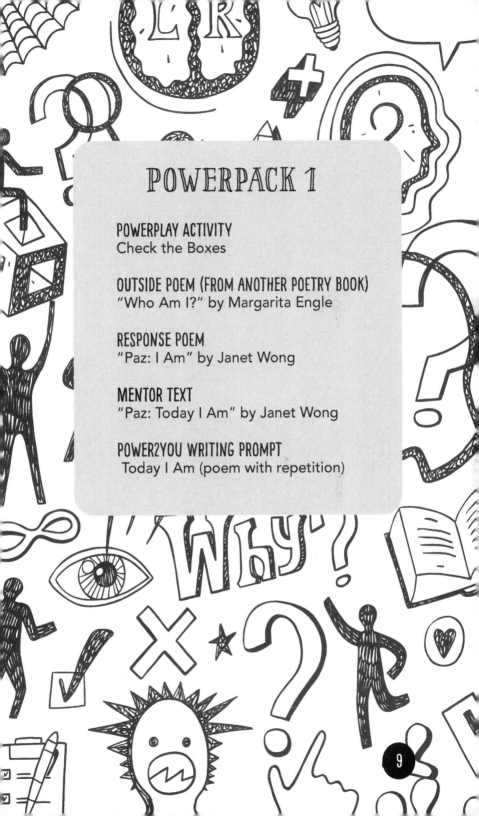

POWERPACK 1

POWERPLAY ACTIVITY
Check the Boxes

OUTSIDE POEM (FROM ANOTHER POETRY BOOK)
"Who Am I?" by Margarita Engle

RESPONSE POEM
"Paz: I Am" by Janet Wong

MENTOR TEXT
"Paz: Today I Am" by Janet Wong

POWER2YOU WRITING PROMPT
Today I Am (poem with repetition)

POWERPLAY

CHECK THE BOXES

Check all the boxes that are true for you
or for someone who is special to you.

☐ Athlete   ☐ Native American

☐ Cousin   ☐ Writer

☐ Vegetarian   ☐ Sister

☐ Redhead   ☐ Runner

☐ Hispanic   ☐ Yoga fan

☐ Boy   ☐ Tech whiz

☐ Teen   ☐ Chess player

☐ Friend   ☐ Girl

☐ Asian   ☐ Church goer

☐ Movie lover   ☐ Brother

- [ ] Gamer
- [ ] Goth
- [ ] Tall
- [ ] Believer
- [ ] Scout
- [ ] African American
- [ ] Singer
- [ ] Reader
- [ ] White
- [ ] Math whiz

- [ ] Petite
- [ ] Chef
- [ ] Hiker
- [ ] Musician
- [ ] LGBTQ
- [ ] Sports fan
- [ ] Band member
- [ ] Cheerleader
- [ ] Artist
- [ ] Black

- [ ] And: _____
- [ ] Plus: _____
- [ ] Also: _____

WHO AM I?
BY MARGARITA ENGLE

Each time I have to fill out a form
that demands my ethnic origin, I try
to do the math. Half this, half that,
with grandparents who were probably
half something else, or maybe
a quarter,
or an eighth.

Why do forms always ask
what I am, instead of asking
who?

PAZ:
I AM

I am a runner.
I am a soccer player,
sister to Joe, a basketball star.
I like to dream of myself
making it far,
a future scientist.
A Nobel winner.
Why not me?

But wait—
this form doesn't really care
about who I really am
and what I do or don't do—

all this form wants to know is:
what kind of
other
are YOU?

PAZ:
TODAY I AM

Today
I am
someone who ate ice cream for breakfast
someone who dresses like a panda (black and white)
someone who hates the smell of banana peels in the class trash
someone who carries way too much in my backpack
someone who carries way too much in my head

TODAY I AM

(poem with repetition)

Now describe yourself using the same poem skeleton, but filling in words and details that apply to you to create a new poem.

TODAY I AM

Today

I am

someone who

someone who

someone who

someone who

someone who

POWERPACK 2

POWERPLAY ACTIVITY
Pick a Number

OUTSIDE POEM (FROM ANOTHER POETRY BOOK)
"Locker Ness Monster" by Robyn Hood Black

RESPONSE POEM
"Paz: Locked Out and Running Late" by Janet Wong

MENTOR TEXT
"Paz: Numbers" by Janet Wong

POWER2YOU WRITING PROMPT
 Numbers (number poem)

PICK A NUMBER

Do you have a locker combination or a lucky number? Add and then color in YOUR numbers below. Or fill in the circles with letters to form a word. Or connect the dots in numerical order.

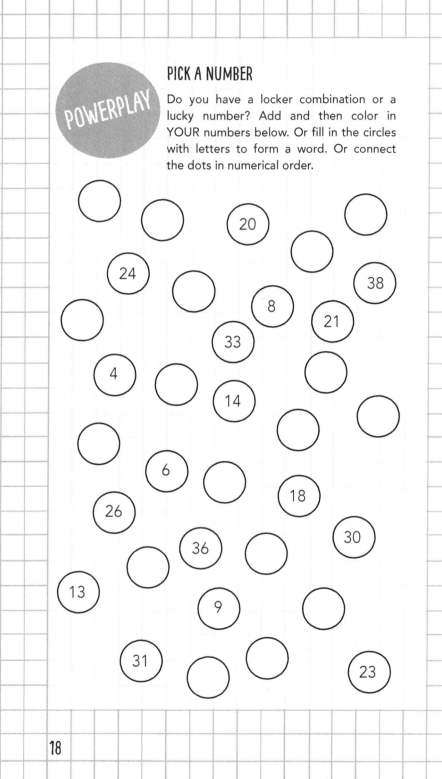

POWERPLAY

20
24
38
8
21
33
4
14
6
18
26
30
36
13
9
31
23

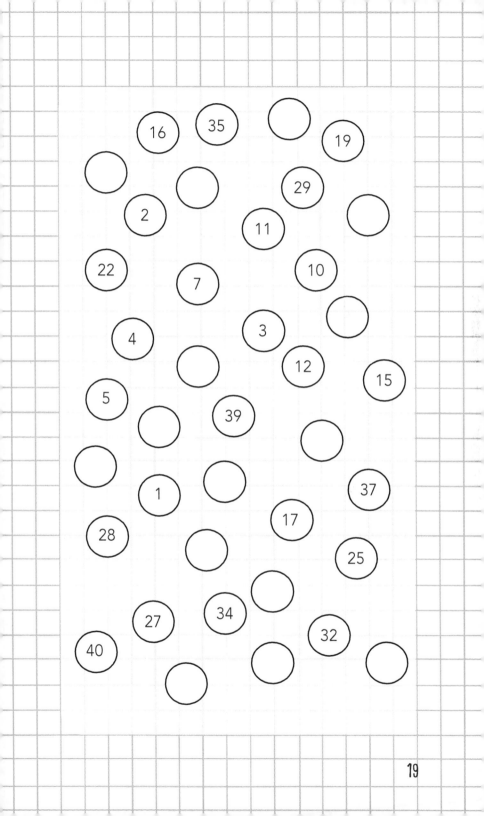

LOCKER NESS MONSTER
BY ROBYN HOOD BLACK

Twenty-four
Eighteen
Six.

Arrrgh. That's not it.

Twenty-six
Fourteen
Eight.

Nothing. Nada. Nyet.

Twenty-six
Eighteen
Four.

CLICK. *That's it!*

Unlock your head,
then your fingers,
then the door.

PAZ:
LOCKED OUT AND RUNNING LATE

Usually I refuse to check a box.
I just let myself be blank.

But today I checked Other
and Hispanic and Asian

to get things over with because
I am in too much of a hurry

and who I really am
this very second is

locked out
and running late.

PAZ:
NUMBERS

4	People would never guess
7	that my mind is such a mess
2	with numbers.
6	But I can memorize a poem,
9	read and read it to make it my own.
9	And then I can use it like a code.
3	Here's a rhyme
4	when it comes time
7	to know my number. OK, let's see:
3	(472) 699-3473!

NUMBERS

(number poem)

Write your telephone number in a vertical column below. Then create a poem by writing a line for each number, adding that number of words in each line (so 9 = 9 words, 7 = 7 words), 2 = 2 words, and so on). Or use another set of numbers that means something special to you.

___

___

___

___

___

___

___

___

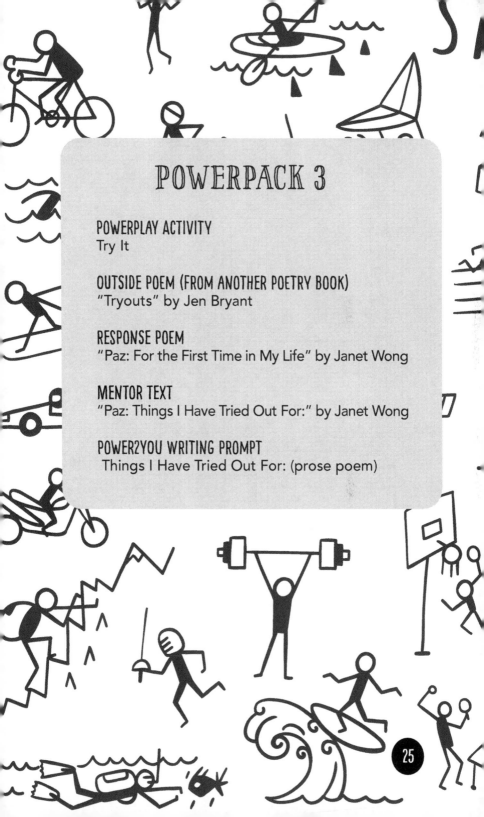

POWERPACK 3

POWERPLAY ACTIVITY
Try It

OUTSIDE POEM (FROM ANOTHER POETRY BOOK)
"Tryouts" by Jen Bryant

RESPONSE POEM
"Paz: For the First Time in My Life" by Janet Wong

MENTOR TEXT
"Paz: Things I Have Tried Out For:" by Janet Wong

POWER2YOU WRITING PROMPT
Things I Have Tried Out For: (prose poem)

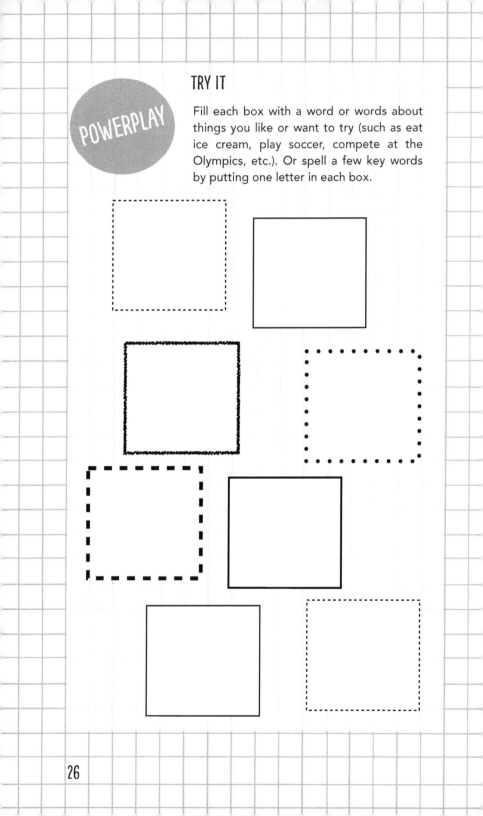

POWERPLAY

TRY IT

Fill each box with a word or words about things you like or want to try (such as eat ice cream, play soccer, compete at the Olympics, etc.). Or spell a few key words by putting one letter in each box.

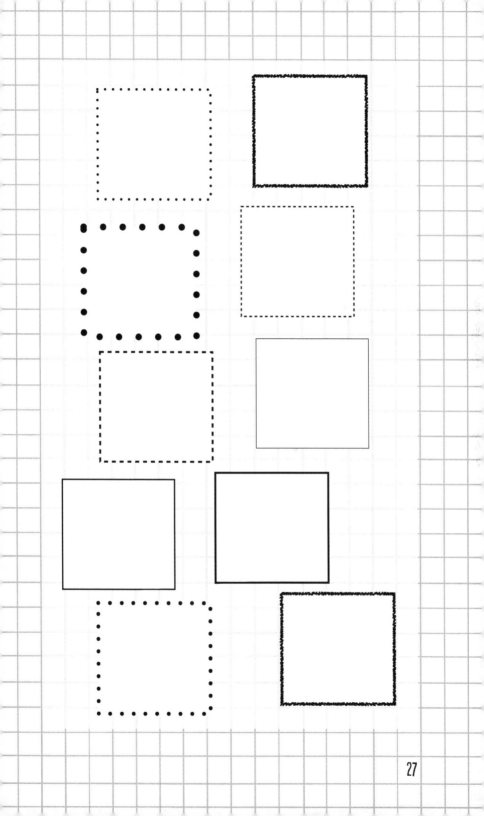

TRYOUTS
BY JEN BRYANT

Thirty-two players
for sixteen spots.
My hands are sweaty,
my stomach's in knots.

See these cones?
Dribble around, then stop.
Pass off to the left,
then take a shot . . .

On your mark, I get set
for the timed shuttle run—
back and forth, back and forth
(listen for the gun).

OK girls, here's what you'll do.
Now count off: One-Two . . .
Face your opponent,
tackle, turn, sprint through.

We line up for long balls,
headers, corner kicks;
the whole time I'm praying
my name will make his list.

PAZ:
FOR THE FIRST TIME IN MY LIFE

They pretend these are true tryouts
but there is just one unclaimed spot
left for someone brand new on our team.

Our team is the best in the state,
made up of all juniors and seniors
except for the coach's daughter.

After the tryouts
for the first time in my life
I can't eat.

After dinner I can't sleep,
a video stuck on loop in my mind
playing and
playing and
playing my bad moves
(never replaying my one good move)

only bad to
worse to
embarrassing to
horrible to
Does she even know how to play this game?

PAZ:
THINGS I HAVE TRIED OUT FOR:

Things I have tried out for:
    the school play
    class vice-president
        (almost got elected)
    soccer team

The school play:
When I was seven years old, I wanted to be the princess in the school play. I really didn't want to be the princess—my cousin Lucesita thought I should be the princess because she wanted to be the queen and she wanted to boss me around. They said my hair was not long enough. I don't understand why a princess needs to have long hair, but I didn't fight it because I thought it would be more fun to be a knight. Or a farmer. Or a dancer. The part I got: the dog. (Well, I am really good at barking.)

THINGS I HAVE TRIED OUT FOR:

(prose poem)

Make a list of things that you have tried or tried out for.

1.

2.

3.

more?

Now choose one of those things on the list and write a short prose poem telling the story behind it.

natural food

water

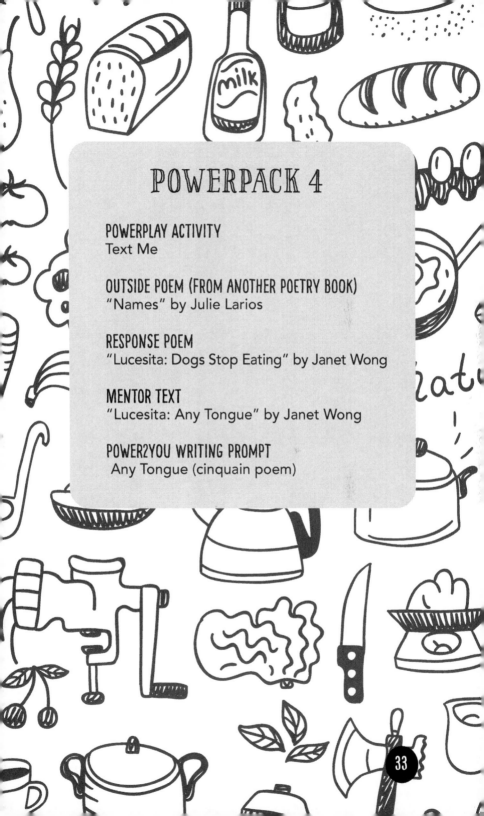

POWERPACK 4

POWERPLAY ACTIVITY
Text Me

OUTSIDE POEM (FROM ANOTHER POETRY BOOK)
"Names" by Julie Larios

RESPONSE POEM
"Lucesita: Dogs Stop Eating" by Janet Wong

MENTOR TEXT
"Lucesita: Any Tongue" by Janet Wong

POWER2YOU WRITING PROMPT
Any Tongue (cinquain poem)

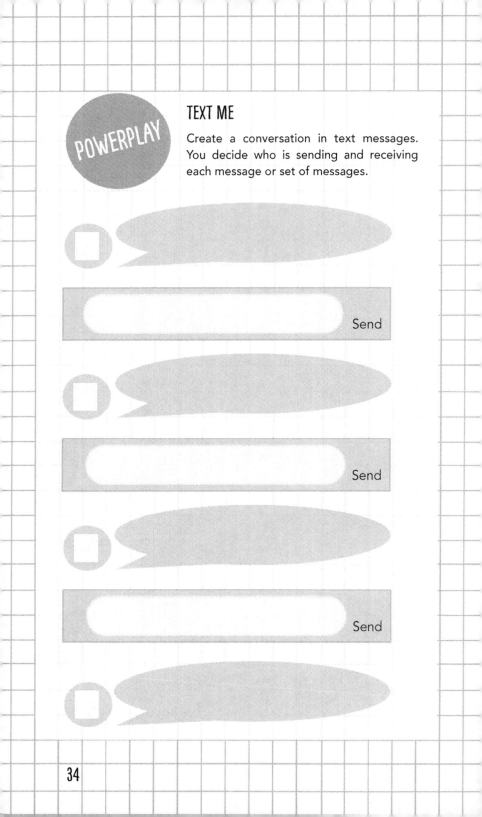

POWERPLAY

TEXT ME

Create a conversation in text messages. You decide who is sending and receiving each message or set of messages.

Send

Send

Send

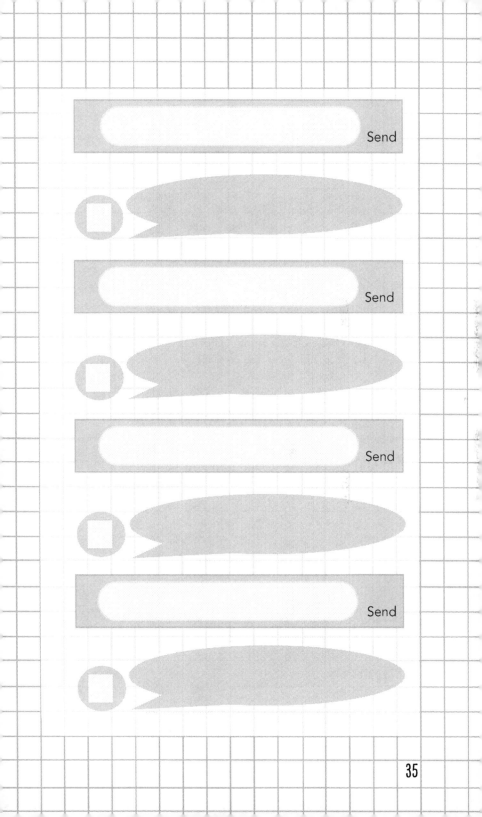

NAMES
BY JULIE LARIOS

Saturday morning means I buy pan dulce
with Tio Chepe and my cousin Lucesita
whose name means "Little Light"—
that's what I call her, and she laughs
and pinches me and calls me "Peace"
because my name is Paz.

In the panaderia even the pastries
have names that mean other things:
Little Horns, Little Shells, Sandals,
Bowties, Braids, and Coco Cookies,
Little Corn, Little Pigs—
everything in Spanish sounds like a song:
Cuernitos, Conchitas, Huaraches, Corbatas,
Trenzas, Cocadas, Elotitos, Cochinitos.

Saturday mornings, Saturday mornings,
that's what I sing because I love pan dulce
and sometimes English can be a song, too.
Tio Chepe, Tio Chepe, Uncle Joey, Uncle Joey,
buy me, please, an Ojo de Buey,
the Eye of a Bull on a Saturday morning!

Tio Chepe picks out a bagful—
this one, that one, that one, this one,
while I sing, and Little Light flirts
with the boy behind the counter
whose name is Jesus.

Note: To hear words and names in "Names" by Julie Larios—and
to experience stepping inside a panaderia (bakery) to buy pan dulce
(pastries)—watch these videos:

"Names" by Julie Larios, read by Priscilla Pineda:
https://www.youtube.com/watch?v=o282Bq-_iCo

"Names" by Julie Larios, read by the poet for No Water River:
https://www.youtube.com/watch?v=iVsrljSRJCc

LUCESITA:
DOGS STOP EATING

Why are you not eating the ppang?
I like to show my cousin Paz now and then
that I know some Korean words too—

words my Auntie Sunny taught me.
It's extra convenient when the Korean word
sounds almost like the word in Spanish.

We're more alike than people think,
Latinos and Asians, especially when
it comes to eating.

I offer Paz another piece of pan dulce
and she shakes her head no again.
Dogs stop eating when they are going to die.

If she is going to die now, just up and go,
I want Paz to know I am taking
our grandmother's pearl mirror.

Note: To hear the Korean word for bread (ppang; sometimes spelled
and pronounced bbang), you can watch this video by Maangchi on
making bread rolls (Roll-ppang), found here:

> http://www.maangchi.com/recipe/bread-rolls
> https://www.youtube.com/watch?v=T8NVqDQZWgk

And here's a fun video by Gochujang Mama (with footage featuring
a panaderia where her husband and son choose pan dulce starting
at the 4-minute mark):

> "Korean Husband Eats Mexican Food":
> https://www.youtube.com/watch?v=MDsZ7NeS0ws

As Gochujang Mama, her husband, and their child say at the
8-minute mark in that video:

> *Mas-isseoyo! Sabroso! Delicious!*

LUCESITA:
ANY TONGUE

Paz and
I play a game
where we text each other
a country and a kind of food.
Japan:

sushi.
Vietnam: pho.
Guatemala: paches!
My aunt says: *Guts are polyglots*
because

tasty
is tasty in
any language, any
tongue, and a burp always means *Oh
That's Good.*

Note: *polyglot* means "knowing several languages"

ANY TONGUE

(cinquain poem)

Write a cinquain (or string a few cinquains together) featuring your favorite foods or foods you would like to try or places you would like to visit. As a reminder, a cinquain is a five-line unrhymed poem made of lines with two, four, six, eight, and two syllables (in that order).

[Two syllables]

[Four syllables]

[Six syllables]

[Eight syllables]

[Two syllables]

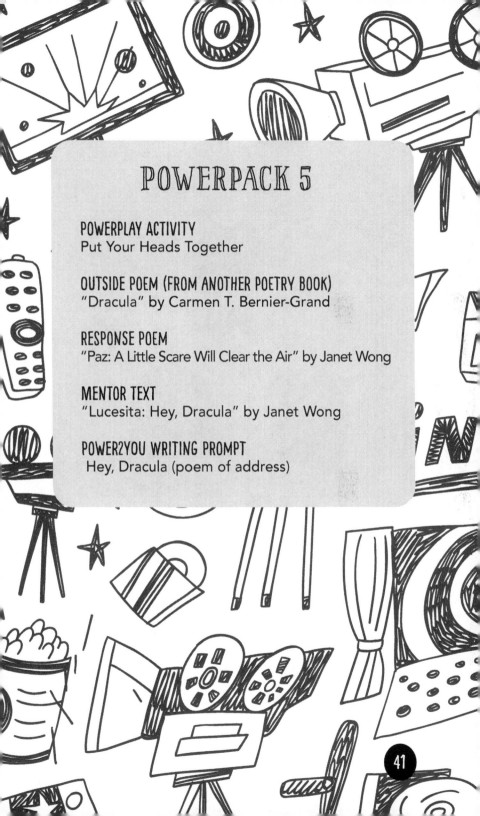

POWERPACK 5

POWERPLAY ACTIVITY
Put Your Heads Together

OUTSIDE POEM (FROM ANOTHER POETRY BOOK)
"Dracula" by Carmen T. Bernier-Grand

RESPONSE POEM
"Paz: A Little Scare Will Clear the Air" by Janet Wong

MENTOR TEXT
"Lucesita: Hey, Dracula" by Janet Wong

POWER2YOU WRITING PROMPT
Hey, Dracula (poem of address)

PUT YOUR HEADS TOGETHER

Create comic or graphic novel panels showing what two friends might be saying to each other at the movies, or imagine other possible dialogue between two people.

DRACULA
BY CARMEN T. BERNIER-GRAND

My sister Lisette loves vampire movies.
We enter the theater
when the movie is a quarter of the way.
When Dracula is about to bite
the pretty lady's neck,
my sister covers her eyes with her hands.
"Tell me when Dracula is gone," she says.
"Shush!" somebody says from the back.
I nudge her with my elbow
when Dracula is gone.
"What happened?" Lisette asks.
"Shh!" says the person in back again.
"Did Dracula bite her neck?"
"No," I say. "She was wearing a cross."
"Shh!"
When the movie ends,
we stay in our seats
to watch the first quarter we missed.

PAZ:
A LITTLE SCARE WILL CLEAR THE AIR

I am too nervous to eat,
too worried about making the team—or not.
Seems my cousin Lucesita thought I was dying
because I didn't gobble down the pan dulce.

But after she figured
that I was not dying
this afternoon—
because it would really stink
to go to a movie with your cousin
and have her die in the middle of it—

Lucesita decided
that we were going to see *Dracula.*
I hate scary movies
but not as much as I hate it
when people sitting near me at the movies
talk all the way through—*Shush!*
This movie drove me nuts.

After the movie
Lucesita is still stuffing her face with pastries.
When I grab a little bit of one
she shouts,
A little scare will clear the air!
This makes everyone stare at her
but she just laughs at that silly rhyme—
laughs and laughs and laughs—
until *oh OH O-H!*
she almost loses
the whole bag of pan dulce.

LUCESITA:
HEY, DRACULA

Hey, Dracula:

Don't bite her neck!
Don't bite her neck!
Don't! DON'T! STOP!

I'm a blood drinker too—
with nosebleeds so bad
the blood slides down your throat
in soft chunks of curdled clots—
so you can believe me when I say
Bloody Mary Mix—
you know, spicy tomato juice?—
tastes so, so much better,
not bitter like blood,
and you won't be burping up the taste
of rust in your mouth for hours.
Skip the lady, Dracula.
Chug down some Bloody Mary Mix,
with a squirt of sour lemon—

No no NO! S-T-O-P!
euwwwwwww

Did you really have to do that?

HEY, DRACULA

(poem of address)

We all like to yell at the TV or movie screen when we see something surprising, right? Write an "apostrophe poem" or "poem of address" to a movie character or television character or game character (e.g., Dracula).

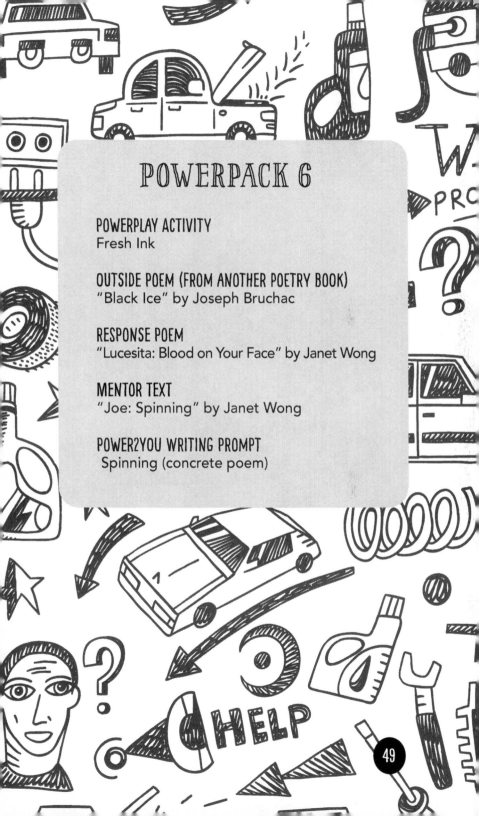

POWERPACK 6

POWERPLAY ACTIVITY
Fresh Ink

OUTSIDE POEM (FROM ANOTHER POETRY BOOK)
"Black Ice" by Joseph Bruchac

RESPONSE POEM
"Lucesita: Blood on Your Face" by Janet Wong

MENTOR TEXT
"Joe: Spinning" by Janet Wong

POWER2YOU WRITING PROMPT
 Spinning (concrete poem)

FRESH INK

What do you see when you look at this inkblot?

Create an inkblot of your own on this page. Fold the page in half down the middle, open it up, scribble on one side with a wet marker, and then quickly fold in half and press down.

Let it dry and then fill in the white spaces with words.

Or describe what you see in your inkblot image.

BLACK ICE
BY JOSEPH BRUCHAC

The whirl of winter wind
slicked the road surface
black and shiny as an otter's back.

The turn of the season's wheel
caught tire treads and heart
at the same time-stopped moment.

I spun, less like a top
than a whirligig beetle,
caromed into the kiss
of guardrail against bumper
rebounded and stopped
just at the edge.

Then the only breath
left held in my chest
was released at last
to spread its wings,
a bird of thanks.

LUCESITA:
BLOOD ON YOUR FACE

I love to be scared.
NOT

real-life scared,
like last winter
when Cousin Joe got his license and
took us out the same day and
spun out of control in the rain and
I thought we were going to be
smashed flat by a semi—

I didn't love that.

And once I start driving
I hope I never get stuck someplace,
broken down and all alone, when—
AAAAAAAAAAAAAAHHH!

But I love to be
fake movie-scared
with other people's
fake blood and fake guts all over the place—

and when the lights go up
there's no blood on your face.
Just butter.

JOE:
SPINNING

y e a h
when a car spins
it's like those teacups at
Disneyland or beetles on their
backs in a puddle of water or or or or or
little plastic tops with crazy spin designs on
colorful paper stickers that are peeling off at the
edges or the wheels of my old busted bicycle from
the time I went off a hill and crash-landed and got
a bunch of rocks stuck under my skin or the hot hot
hot hot soup I stir until it makes a tornado in the bowl
spinning spinning spinning spinning like Earth spins
spinning like the neighbor twins skating in the street
spinning fast like Grandma's fancy washing machine
when she puts it on the super-dirty-smelly setting
spinning slow like the dryer so hot and exhausted
spinning slow real slow like I want to dance with
you-know-who except I'm not sure she likes
me even if my sister Paz is always saying
She likes you, Joe, can't you tell? Well,
uh, no, I can't tell because my mind
has been spinning and spinning
and is done spun
o u t

SPINNING

(concrete poem)

What else can you think of that might be in the shape of a circle or sphere?
- A soccer ball
- A doughnut
- A pizza
- A coin
- A dance
- A bug's flight

Write a concrete or "shape" poem about something round or circular or spherical and try to arrange your words or lines in the shape of a circle or ring.

Or try a different shape, if you prefer.

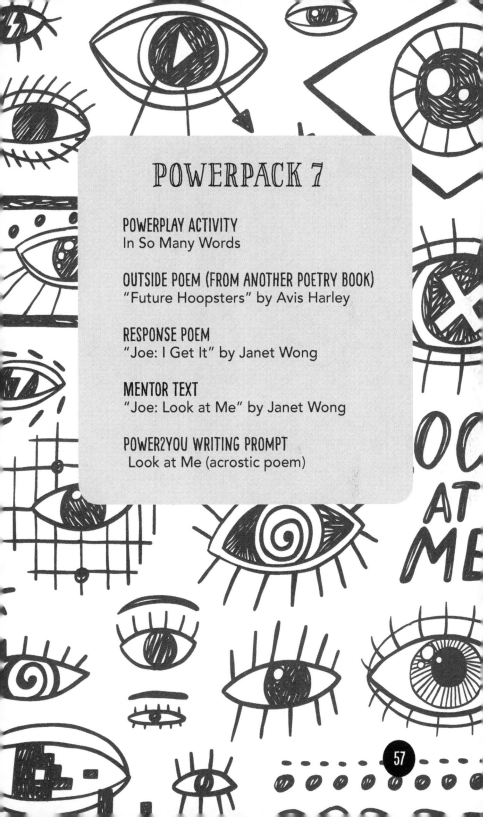

POWERPACK 7

POWERPLAY ACTIVITY
In So Many Words

OUTSIDE POEM (FROM ANOTHER POETRY BOOK)
"Future Hoopsters" by Avis Harley

RESPONSE POEM
"Joe: I Get It" by Janet Wong

MENTOR TEXT
"Joe: Look at Me" by Janet Wong

POWER2YOU WRITING PROMPT
Look at Me (acrostic poem)

POWERPLAY

IN SO MANY WORDS

These are some of the words we use most often. Circle the ones you like best. Or black out all the words you don't like.

the	and	a	have	I
it	for	not	he	you
do	but	his	they	we
say	her	she	will	us
there	what	so	up	out
child	if	who	go	me
use	make	can	like	time
no	just	know	take	year
life	good	then	most	any
people	see	other	now	look
only	eye	come	over	new
think	also	back	after	any
place	two	how	our	man
work	first	well	way	day
hand	even	want	because	fly
these	give	world	woman	box

week	point	group	tell	call
number	find	feel	try	car
leave	fact	last	great	long
little	person	high	small	next
young	public	bad	same	able
music	paper	river	mile	until
example	care	mark	book	walk
begin	carry	rain	eat	dog
room	friend	idea	fish	feet
north	once	hear	cut	sure
watch	color	face	decide	ten
enough	different	girl	boy	war
usual	ready	ever	list	fire
body	family	question	pose	rock
told	problem	king	better	best
remember	interest	reach	sing	love
listen	voice	simple	money	star
power	fine	beauty	teach	big
sleep	warm	nothing	child	hand

FUTURE HOOPSTERS
BY AVIS HARLEY

Hour after hour
Out in the park
Or in the back lane
Playing till dark,
Shooting
The ball for that net reward—
Echoes of
Rebounds sound off the board!

Honing
Our skills,
Perfecting the aim—
Embracing the dream that
Shines through the game.

JOE:
I GET IT

I get it.
I know what Paz is going through.

I know what it means to win.
I know what it means to fit in,
to belong to a team,
the best team,
to have a dream.

Someday I'll play in the NBA.

Well, probably not.

But
as long as
they call me
Little Steph
I can hope.

JOE:
LOOK AT ME

Be yourself, Coach tells me.
A natural athlete like you can be a
Success on any team, but not if you play like a lazy
Kid: You've got to activate your eyes,
Engage your brain, see every little thing on
The court—don't look down. Use your eyes, use your
Brain, see the whole court. You're smart, so
Act smart. You listening to me? Look at me! Play
Like your feet are on fire. Play like there's
Lightning in your pocket. Got it?

LOOK AT ME

(acrostic poem)

POWER 2 YOU

Now try writing in the form of an acrostic poem. Here, the first letter of each line spells a key word (e.g., basketball). For an extra challenge, you might see if the first WORD in each line can also build a sentence (e.g., Be a success, kid: engage the brain, act like lightning).

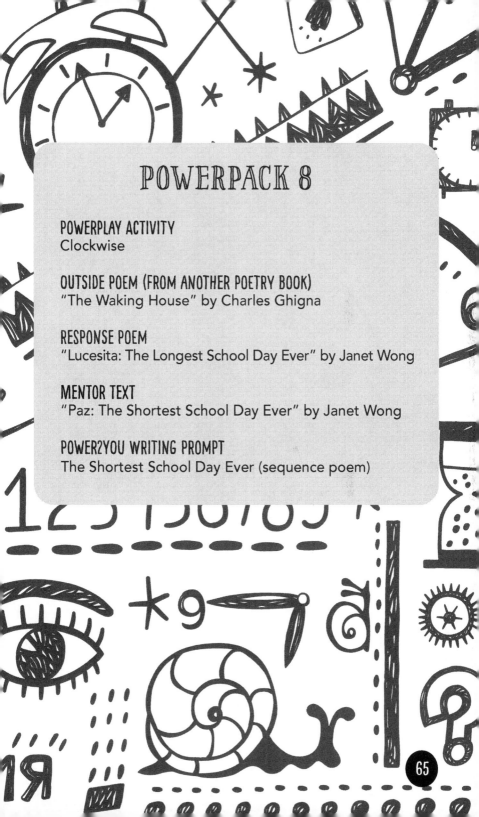

POWERPACK 8

POWERPLAY ACTIVITY
Clockwise

OUTSIDE POEM (FROM ANOTHER POETRY BOOK)
"The Waking House" by Charles Ghigna

RESPONSE POEM
"Lucesita: The Longest School Day Ever" by Janet Wong

MENTOR TEXT
"Paz: The Shortest School Day Ever" by Janet Wong

POWER2YOU WRITING PROMPT
The Shortest School Day Ever (sequence poem)

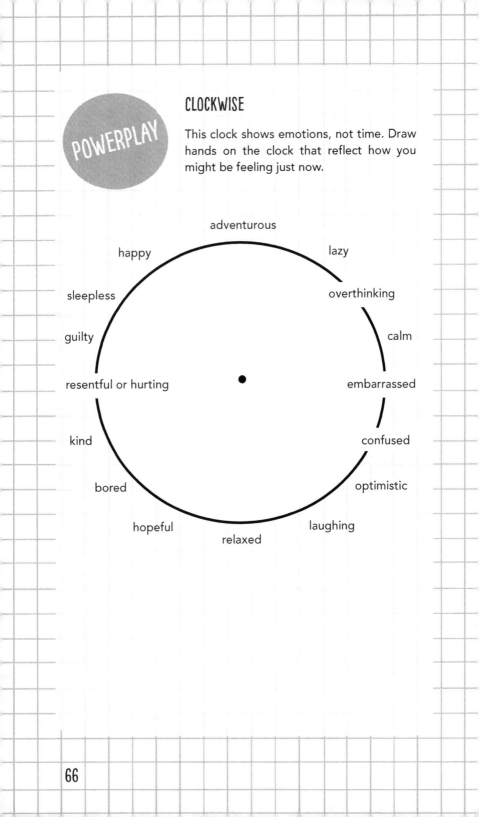

POWERPLAY

CLOCKWISE

This clock shows emotions, not time. Draw hands on the clock that reflect how you might be feeling just now.

adventurous

happy   lazy

sleepless   overthinking

guilty   calm

resentful or hurting   embarrassed

kind   confused

bored   optimistic

hopeful   laughing

relaxed

Forget the numbers on a clock. Create your own emotional clock and add words that describe your own mood, personality, or other emotional possibilities. What does your clock say about you or the people around you?

THE WAKING HOUSE
BY CHARLES GHIGNA

My house wakes me up every morning
Exactly at six forty-five—
That's when my alarm clock starts dancing
And the sounds of my house come alive.

The blow dryer screams at the top of its lungs,
The clothes dryer buzzer starts pinging.
I pull up the covers over my head.
My snooze alarm clock starts singing.

The toaster goes pop. When will it stop?
The tea kettle whistles away.
The microwave beep won't let me sleep,
I might as well join in the day.

LUCESITA:
THE LONGEST SCHOOL DAY EVER

It is the longest school day ever.
9am felt like 7am, I was so tired—
couldn't sleep all night, worrying for Paz.
11am was torture.
I thought of lemons
so I'd have some spit to swallow
to make my rumbling stomach shut up.

Lunch was a rock-hard burrito. I forgot:
never be the first one in line on Monday—
who do you think gets Friday's leftover food?

During drama class after lunch
I started daydreaming and remembered
when our math teacher from last year
turned the longest school day ever
into the shortest and best—snap—just like that.
Maybe if I remember hard enough
it will happen again.

Snap
[waiting]
[waiting]
[waiting]
[waiting]
[waiting]
[waiting]

One of these days.
Maybe.

PAZ:
THE SHORTEST SCHOOL DAY EVER

8am: Homeroom
zzzzzzzzzzzzzzzzz

8:20am:
zzzzzzzzzzzzzzzzzzzzzzzzzzzzzzzzzzzz

9:30am:
zzzzzzzzzzzzzzzzzzzzzzzzzzzzzzzzzz

10:40am:
zzzzzzzzzzzzzzzzzzzzzzzzzzzzzzzzz

11:50am:
Lunch already? How did I get from Homeroom
to 1st period to 2nd period to 3rd then here?

11:53am:
Why is this burrito so hard?

2:44pm:
Huh? Whuh? Sorry, Miss Guadalupe.
Yes, Ma'am.
No, Ma'am.
I am so so so sorry, Ma'am.
A note for me? What did you say?

2:45pm:
OMG HOOOORAY!!!

THE SHORTEST SCHOOL DAY EVER

(sequence poem)

Write a poem with a very strong sequence or time order. You could feature the hours of the day, days of the week, or months of the year—or have a completely different focus, like steps in "how to" do something or driving directions or a slice of history.

POWERPACK 9

POWERPLAY ACTIVITY
This Will Never Fly

OUTSIDE POEM (FROM ANOTHER POETRY BOOK)
"What She Asked" by Virginia Euwer Wolff

RESPONSE POEM
"Lucesita: It's Just the Sun" by Janet Wong

MENTOR TEXT
"Lucesita: Less Pressure (A Found Poem)" by Janet Wong

POWER2YOU WRITING PROMPT
Less Pressure (found poem)

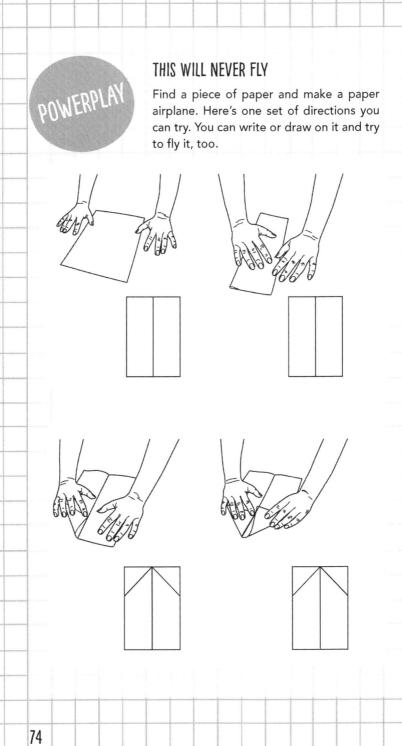

THIS WILL NEVER FLY

Find a piece of paper and make a paper airplane. Here's one set of directions you can try. You can write or draw on it and try to fly it, too.

POWERPLAY

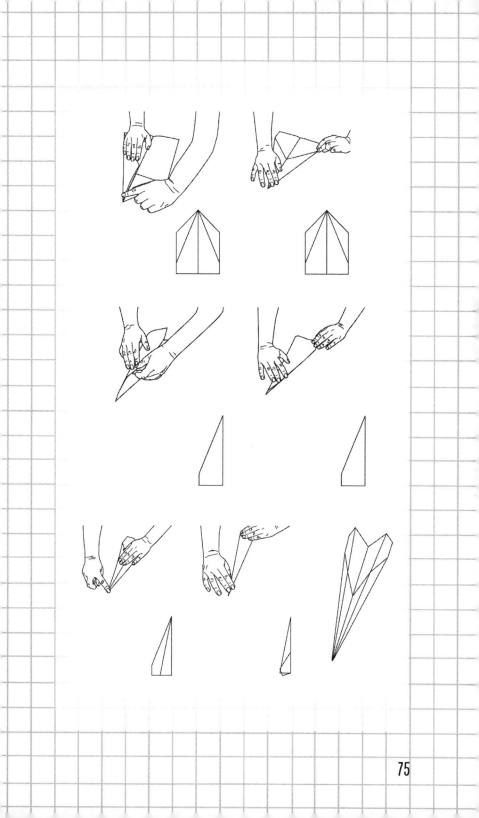

WHAT SHE ASKED
BY VIRGINIA EUWER WOLFF

Remember that classroom afternoon,
every big and little thing
was wrong: sleet outside, radiator clank within,
broken chalk, stubborn pens,
misbehaving software staring back.
The wall told us in its blunt rasp
about another bus delay.
Minds lolling, girls moody, guys grouchy,
we'd have tried on dour if we'd ever heard of it.
Even the boy who was memorizing pi
had dimmed his lights.
Marooned on the crust of that mopey day
our teacher looked around at all 38 of us
and up at the sullen, pocked ceiling squares
and wondered softly,
"Who in this whole room
can fly a paper airplane the highest?"
And every one of us did.

LUCESITA:
IT'S JUST THE SUN

Paz is flying high
because she made the team.
It's like she's on an airplane
headed for an island vacation.

I feel happy for her. Really.
It's just that I feel like
I'm stuck pedaling a rickety old bike
on the way to a factory job.

Hey, she says. *Are you OK?*
Yeah-yeah, I lie, blinking.
It's the sun in my eyes.
It's just the sun.

LUCESITA:
LESS PRESSURE (A FOUND POEM)

How Do an Airplane's Wings Provide Lift?

The shape of an airplane's wings is what makes it able to fly. Airplanes' wings are curved on top and flatter on the bottom. That shape makes air flow over the top faster than under the bottom. So, less air pressure is on top of the wing. This condition makes the wing, and the airplane it's attached to, move up. Using curves to change air pressure is a trick used on many aircraft. Helicopter rotor blades use this trick. Lift for kites also comes from a curved shape. Even sailboats use this concept. A boat's sail is like a wing. That's what makes the sailboat move.

What Is Drag?

Drag is a force that tries to slow something down. It makes it hard for an object to move. It is harder to walk or run through water than through air. That is because water causes more drag than air. The shape of an object also changes the amount of drag. Most round surfaces have less drag than flat ones. Narrow surfaces usually have less drag than wide ones. The more air that hits a surface, the more drag it makes.

—from nasa.gov/audience/forstudents/k-4/stories/nasa-knows/what-is-aerodynamics-k4.html

Less Pressure (A Found Poem)

Over the top pressure.
How to slow down?
The trick:
Change the amount of drag.
Make the move.

LESS PRESSURE
(found poem)

Try writing a "found" poem of your own looking for words from another source and then arranging them into a poem. You can use these paragraphs on airplane wings and drag, if you like. You can use another poem or page from this book. You can use a passage of prose from an online source. Or you can even use text from a cereal box or other source with words on it.

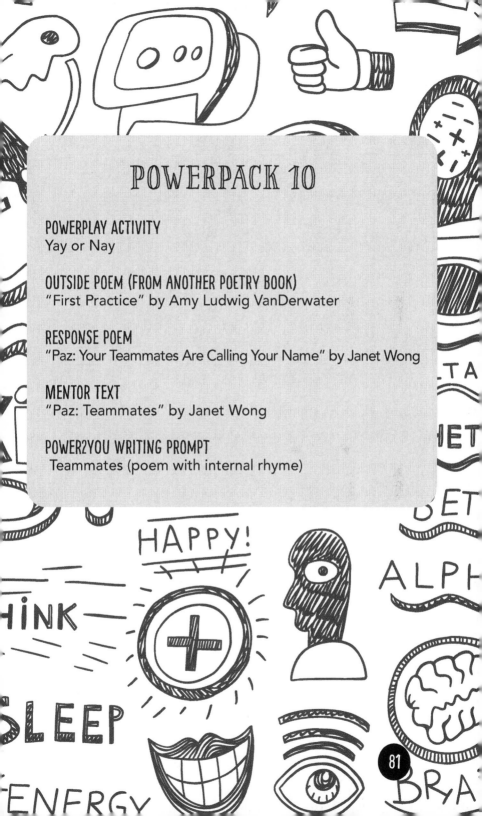

POWERPACK 10

POWERPLAY ACTIVITY
Yay or Nay

OUTSIDE POEM (FROM ANOTHER POETRY BOOK)
"First Practice" by Amy Ludwig VanDerwater

RESPONSE POEM
"Paz: Your Teammates Are Calling Your Name" by Janet Wong

MENTOR TEXT
"Paz: Teammates" by Janet Wong

POWER2YOU WRITING PROMPT
Teammates (poem with internal rhyme)

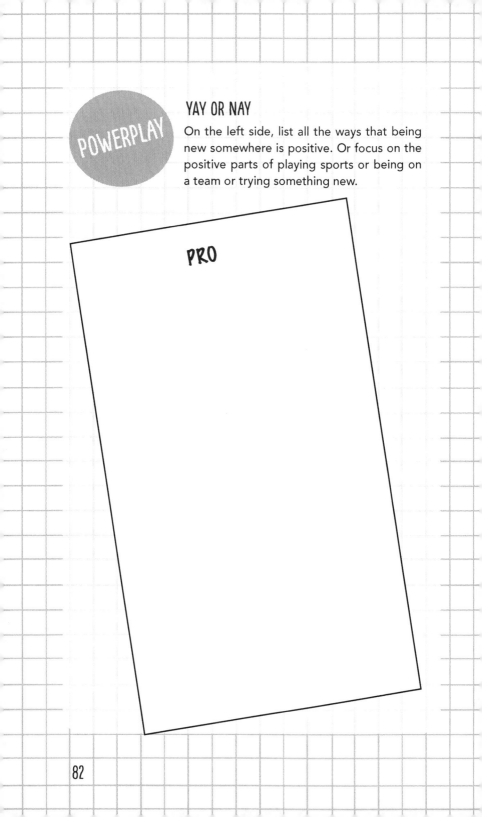

POWERPLAY

YAY OR NAY

On the left side, list all the ways that being new somewhere is positive. Or focus on the positive parts of playing sports or being on a team or trying something new.

PRO

On the right side, list all the negative aspects of being new somewhere. Or focus on the negative aspects of playing sports or being on a team or trying something new.

CON

FIRST PRACTICE
BY AMY LUDWIG VANDERWATER

I'm new on this team
but I've been new before.

It's an in-between place,
an invisible door
that turns outside to inside,
stranger to friend.

It's the first day of practice.

I try to pretend
that my hands are not shaking.
I'm not scared at all.
I'll be tough on the field.
I'll go for the ball.

I'm new
but my teammates
are calling my name.
I've been new before.
I'm good at this game.

PAZ:
YOUR TEAMMATES ARE CALLING YOUR NAME

When your mother whispers your name
you feel loved.

When your brother shouts your name
you still feel loved

after you get over how much you hate it
when everyone looks at you.

When your cousin sings your name Beyoncé-style
you act all girly together and laugh.

When your teammates call your name
after your first goal, you can finally breathe.

PAZ:
TEAMMATES

Being on a team
means
you belong.
Whatever you do,
right or wrong,
you know
your team
will stick by your side.

Being on a team
means
you don't need
to hide your feelings.
You can speak
your mind,
just
don't be mean—

you want to respect,
to honor,
the team.

TEAMMATES

(poem with internal rhyme)

Try writing a poem that uses rhyme in nontraditional ways. Don't limit yourself to regular end rhyme and exact rhyme. Try using irregular rhyme, internal rhyme, or slant or "near" rhyme (e.g., team-means, hide-mind).

POWERPACK 11

POWERPLAY ACTIVITY
Getting Sketchy

OUTSIDE POEM (FROM ANOTHER POETRY BOOK)
"World Cup" by Jen Bryant

RESPONSE POEM
"Lucesita: You Just Wait" by Janet Wong

MENTOR TEXT
"Paz: Ode to the Game" by Janet Wong

POWER2YOU WRITING PROMPT
Ode to the Game (ode poem)

GETTING SKETCHY

Try sketchnoting to fill in each shape with key words, drawings, doodles, lines, and arrows reflecting what you're thinking about just now or the highlights of the year so far or your favorite elementary school memories.

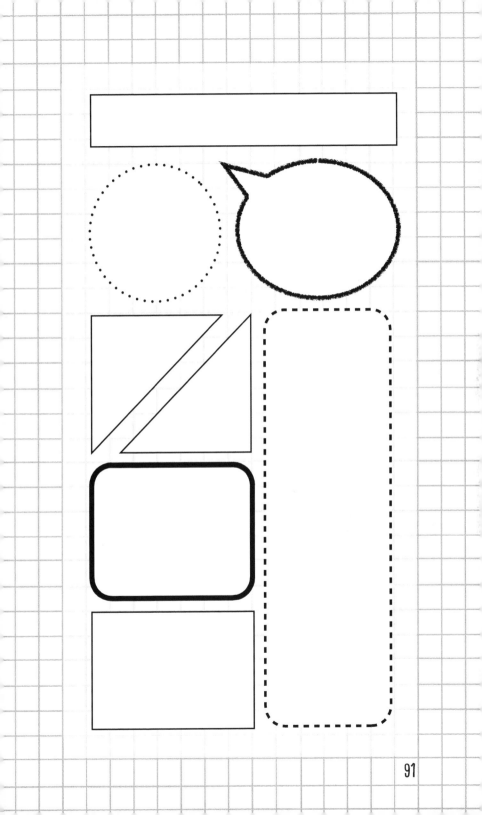

WORLD CUP
BY JEN BRYANT

After practice we walk
      to Megan's house, flop
down on her basement couch
      and watch a taped
World Cup game between
      the American and German women.

Coach points out their great plays:
      see how she was patient there
and didn't shoot too soon?
      and their mistakes:
the defender lost her mark
      did you see that?

We all nod, yes, of course, though
      each of us is daydreaming—
as we watch the passes, shots,
      and corner kicks—
of one day running down that field,
      wearing U. S. A. on our backs.

LUCESITA:
YOU JUST WAIT

Paz is not one of us anymore.
She's on her way to a scholarship, for sure.
Or the Olympics. Or the World Cup.

She's dreaming about it already.
Mama tells me to follow my dreams, too.
I wish I had something to dream about.

You're so pretty, Auntie Sunny says,
you don't need to worry.
Paz can teach you soccer, Tio Chepe says.

Mama says I should write for movies.
Movies are stories. You love telling stories.
She says I'm smart as anybody.

You're going to be so lucky. Watch.
Everything good is going to happen.
You just wait.

PAZ:
ODE TO THE GAME

Soccer is
the smell of the grass
sweating

Soccer is
the sun
melding your muscles together

Soccer is
every single nerve
pulsing as you run so strong

ODE TO THE GAME

(ode poem)

Now try to write an ode of your own. Think of something you love or enjoy and write your poem as a tribute or recognition of those special qualities, experiences, or memories (e.g., soccer).

POWERPACK 12

POWERPLAY ACTIVITY
Me and Mine

OUTSIDE POEM (FROM ANOTHER POETRY BOOK)
"Cousins" by Charles Waters

RESPONSE POEM
"Joe: Wait for Me" by Janet Wong

MENTOR TEXT
"Lucesita: Rising" by Janet Wong

POWER2YOU WRITING PROMPT
Rising (your choice)

ME AND MINE

Forget genealogy and fill in your "family tree" showing your connection with your immediate and extended family members, putting each of them wherever you like. Add or subtract circles and connections, as needed.

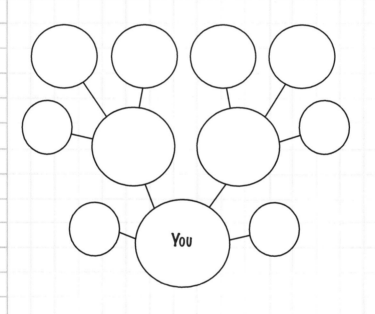

Now make a "friend tree" showing how your friends connect to you. Add or subtract circles and connections, as needed.

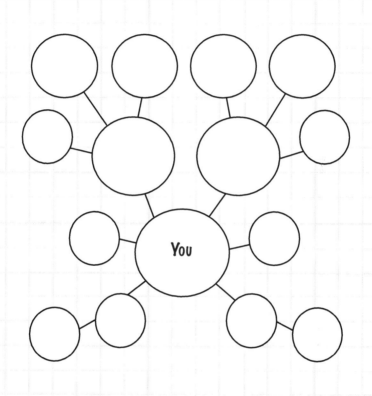

COUSINS
BY CHARLES WATERS

Making breakfast—
Scrambled eggs,

Mosquito bites
On our legs,

Gazing at stars
Until dawn,

Playing soccer
On our lawn:

Every summer
We are free

To rule the world—
You and me.

JOE:
WAIT FOR ME

Our physics teacher said it
and I think it's true:

You feel like
the years are going faster
when you get older
because they really are,
compared to how long you've lived.

The cousins are running around like little kids,
guys slapping each other with towels,
girls snapping silly selfies.
Lucesita is holding hands with Paz and
singing and dancing like Beyoncé.

When I see the cousins crowd in
for the 200th picture

I shout,
Hey, guys—wait for me.

LUCESITA:
RISING

I read somewhere
that Carrie Fisher
(Princess Leia) said:

*Sometimes I feel like I've got my nose
pressed up against the window of a bakery,
only I'm the bread.*

Looking around at us cousins this morning,
I'm thinking we're kind of like bread—
and it's not such a bad thing to be.

Bread fills you up when you're empty.
Wouldn't you rather be bread than crackers?
Crackers are flat and hard. Bread gives.

We cousins are like a box of pan dulce,
some plain, some sweet, some sparkly.
Some like little pigs. But we all give.

Maybe Paz is a little different,
a sprouted multigrain roll,
so healthy and all.

Right now, anyway,
we're just sitting here in the kitchen,
and we're rising. We're rising up.

RISING

(your choice)

You've experimented with rhyme and internal rhyme and repetition. You have focused on numbers and sequence and tried various forms including cinquain, acrostic, shape, found, ode, and apostrophe poems. Now it's your turn to try a poem in any form or with any device that you like. You can continue the story, end it from a different point of view, or change the ending completely. It's up to you!

NOTE:

You can find additional poems about Paz and
Lucesita and Joe, as well as downloadable files
of student activity pages, at PomeloBooks.com.

POETRY
FRIDAY
POWER
RESOURCES

WHAT'S NEXT?

In the pages that follow, you'll find writing tips, suggested publication venues, and helpful websites. There are also recommended books about writing, poetry published by teens, and verse novels and anthologies, as well as talking points and creative ways to perform poems.

Think about sharing your poems during Teen Read Week in the fall, or at an Open House at school, or with friends and family members for a special occasion—or a reason of your own. You might even collaborate with your whole class to choose favorite poems, write original poems to connect into a story, and then perform the story for a public audience.

If you want to try doing a project of your own, we recommend finding poems from either a large anthology of more than a hundred poems or from several smaller books of poetry. You don't want to take an unfair amount of poems from any one book. And whichever books you choose, the important thing is to respect the copyright of the poets involved.

Look for more ideas for expressing yourself through poetry on YouTube or in the PoetryinMotion public poems on mass transit, or create a hallway anthology of favorite poems on your school campus.

You can find long lists of poetry collections and anthologies in *The Poetry Teacher's Book of Lists* by Sylvia Vardell and also at the Poetry for Children blog (PoetryforChildren.Blogspot.com). Some anthologies that we hope you'll consider first for a project are our books in *The Poetry Friday Anthology* series, which you can learn more about at our website, PomeloBooks.com.

12 MORE POEMS
FROM THE POETRY FRIDAY ANTHOLOGY FOR MIDDLE SCHOOL

The story in this book was built upon 12 poems from The Poetry Friday Anthology for Middle School, *written by a variety of poets, plus 24 new poems by Janet Wong. Below is a list of 12 MORE poems (from the same anthology of 110 poems) that you can weave into your own story.*

1. "Bilingual" by Margarita Engle
   *feeling torn between two places, two identities

2. "Racing the Clouds" by Jacqueline Jules
   *the thrill of running before a storm

3. "Restless" by Joyce Sidman
   *imagine being somewhere else right now

4. "Lost" by Kate Coombs
   *hurting a friend's feelings

5. "Silence" by Linda Kulp
   *getting caught texting at school

6. "The Fear Factor" by Sara Holbrook
   *will courage be there when you need it?

7. "In Case You're Reading My Journal" by Betsy Franco
   *sharing mixed-up, private feelings

8. "Saying No" by Amy Ludwig VanDerwater
   *when your family teases you about being vegetarian

9. "Safe in My Shell" by Ann Whitford Paul
   *feeling too shy and anxious to reach out

10. "Sitting for Trishie Devlin" by Sonya Sones
    *the fun of babysitting

11. "Look My Way" by Robyn Hood Black
    *when you want your crush to look at you

12. "The Boy" by Guadalupe Garcia McCall
    *when someone likes you, but your dad doesn't approve

POETRY WRITING CHECKLIST

Poets of all ages often need guidance in looking at their own work critically. A checklist or guidelines can be helpful in developing skill in revising one's own writing. No single list is perfect, nor is each step necessary every time, but such checklists can be a good tool. Here is one example with a dozen questions that you might find helpful, created by poet and poetry teacher Sara Holbrook.

HOLBROOK'S SELF-EDIT CHECKLIST

1. Have I written from one point of view?
2. Have I narrowed the focus?
3. Have I defined all of my opinion words?
4. Have I double-checked the basics (like subject-verb agreement, verb tense, spelling)?
5. Have I worked to get the trite out (of overused words and phrases)?
6. Have I practiced cutting out excess words (like articles)?
7. Have I read the poem aloud to see if it flows and makes sense?
8. Does the poem contain any fake rhymes (a rhyme used for the rhyme's sake, rather than for the sake of the message)?
9. Have I used action verbs to clarify images?
10. Was I consistent with the pattern I chose?
11. Did I maintain a clear and consistent image?
12. Have I shared my poem with another person? (It shouldn't need explaining.)

Based on: Holbrook, Sara. 2005. *Practical Poetry: A Nonstandard Approach to Meeting Content-Area Standards.* Portsmouth, NH: Heinemann, p. 54-56.

PLACES TO PUBLISH YOUR POETRY

Here are a variety of print and online sources that include poetry by young writers. Be sure to check the rules and specifications for submitting in each venue. Give it a try, have fun, and good luck!

Creative Kids (ages 8-16)   http://www.ckmagazine.org
*"the nation's largest magazine for and by kids"

Teen Ink (grades 7-12)   http://www.teenink.com
*teenage writing, art, photos, and national forums

Carus Publishing (Cicada, Cobblestone, Faces, Dig, Muse)
(ages 9-14+)   http://www.cobblestonepub.com/index.html
*magazines on topics from nature to history and more

New Moon: The Magazine for Girls and Their Dreams (ages 8-14)
http://www.newmoon.com/
*special online community and magazine for girls

Skipping Stones (all ages)   http://www.skippingstones.org
*international, multicultural, environmental magazine

Merlyn's Pen (grades 6-12)   http://www.merlynspen.com
*"fiction, essays, and poems by America's teens"

The Claremont Review (ages 13-19)
http://www.theclaremontreview.ca
*international magazine based in Canada

Stone Soup (ages 8-13)   http://stonesoup.com
*stories, poems, book reviews, and artwork by young people

The Telling Room (ages 6-18)
http://www.tellingroom.org/stories
*publications of annual anthologies, chapbooks, and on the web

Canvas (ages 8-13)   http://canvasliteraryjournal.com
*published in print, ebook, web, video, and audio formats

Writing (grades 7-12)
http://classroommagazines.scholastic.com
*monthly publication, writing prompts and writing contests

BOOKS ABOUT WRITING POETRY

Several poets have written books for young people ABOUT poetry writing. Here are resources that you may find helpful.

1. Appelt, Kathi. 2002. *Poems from Homeroom: A Writer's Place to Start.* Henry Holt. *Appelt combines her original poems with ideas and creative writing exercises

2. Fletcher, Ralph J. 2001. *A Writer's Notebook: Unlocking the Writer Within You.* HarperTrophy. *Advice on how to keep notes and then turn them into stories and poems

3. Fletcher, Ralph J. 2002. *Poetry Matters: Writing a Poem from the Inside Out.* HarperCollins. *a practical guide to creating poetry, complete with interviews with poets

4. Holbrook, Sara and Salinger, Michael. 2006. *Outspoken! How to Improve Writing and Speaking Skills through Poetry Performance.* Heinemann. *a fun and conversational guide

5. Janeczko, Paul B., comp. 2002. *Seeing the Blue Between: Advice and Inspiration for Young Poets.* Candlewick. *a poetry collection with poems and advice from 32 poets

6. Kapell, Dave and Steenland, Sally. 1998. *Kids' Magnetic Poetry Book and Creativity Kit.* Workman. *tips and tools for making poetry creation fun and game-like

7. Lawson, JonArno. 2008. *Inside Out: Children's Poets Discuss Their Work.* Walker. *23 poets share poems and then explain how the poem came to be

8. Prelutsky, Jack. 2008. *Pizza, Pigs, and Poetry: How to Write a Poem.* Greenwillow. *the poet shares how he creates poems from anecdotes, often using comic exaggeration

9. Salas, Laura Purdie. 2011. *Picture Yourself Writing Poetry: Using Photos to Inspire Writing.* Capstone. *a clear and engaging approach with writing prompts and mentor texts

10. Wolf, Allan. 2006. *Immersed in Verse: An Informative, Slightly Irreverent & Totally Tremendous Guide to Living the Poet's Life.* Sterling. *a witty guide for "going gonzo over words"

BOOKS WITH POEMS BY TEENS

Here are several notable collections of poetry written by young people.

1. Aguado, Bill. Ed. 2003. *Paint Me Like I Am.* Harper. *raw and honest poems explore identity, creativity, and relationships

2. Franco, Betsy. 2001. Ed. *Things I Have to Tell You: Poems and Writing by Teenage Girls.* Candlewick. *teen girls offer prose and poems about sexuality, identity, fears, dreams, and angst

3. Franco, Betsy. 2001. Ed. *You Hear Me? Poems and Writing by Teenage Boys.* Candlewick. *prose and poetry by teen boys explore angry and honest emotions and experiences

4. Franco, Betsy. 2008. Ed. *Falling Hard: 100 Love Poems by Teenagers.* Candlewick. *honest poems about love by teens from many different backgrounds and sexual orientations

5. Johnson, Dave. Ed. 2000. *Movin': Teen Poets Take Voice.* Orchard. *teens write about real life in poetic and evocative language

6. Lyne, Sandford. Ed. 2004. *Soft Hay Will Catch You.* Simon & Schuster. *Kentucky poet Lyne gathers teen poems about the search for self, home and family, and connections to place

7. McLaughlin, Timothy. Ed. 2012. *Walking on Earth and Touching the Sky: Poetry and Prose by Lakota Youth at Red Cloud Indian School.* Abrams. *powerful prose and poetry by Lakota students at Red Cloud Indian School in South Dakota

8. Nye, Naomi Shihab. Ed. 2000. *Salting the Ocean: 100 Poems by Young Poets.* Greenwillow. *Nye collected "100 poems by 100 poets in grades one through twelve"

9. Tom, Karen, and Kiki. 2001. *Angst! Teen Verses from the Edge.* Workman. *girls share edgy thoughts and frustrations

10. WritersCorps. 2008. *Tell the World.* HarperCollins. *a cross-section of teen voices sharing slices of teenage life

POETRY COLLECTIONS WITH POEMS BY INDIVIDUAL POETS

In these books, all the poems are by the same poet, even if they pursue a variety of themes or topics.

1. Adoff, Arnold. 2010. *Roots and Blues: A Celebration.* Boston: Houghton Mifflin Harcourt. *poems and paintings celebrate the culture and history of blues music

2. Hopkins, Lee Bennett. 1995. *Been to Yesterdays: Poems of a Life.* WordSong/Boyds Mills. *powerful autobiographical poems about family and becoming a writer

3. Hughes, Langston. (75th anniversary edition) 2007. *The Dream Keeper.* Knopf. *originally published in 1932, this landmark work still speaks to readers today about the human experience

4. Mora, Pat. 2010. *Dizzy in Your Eyes.* Knopf. *all kinds of love (romantic, familial, platonic) celebrated in poems in many forms

5. Nye, Naomi Shihab. 2005. *A Maze Me: Poems for Girls.* Greenwillow. *thoughtful poems about "growing up girl" and coping with love, friendship, body image, hopes

6. Park, Linda Sue. 2007. *Tap Dancing on the Roof: Sijo Poems.* Clarion. *a smart and appealing introduction to sijo poems, a traditional Korean verse form with an ironic twist at the end

7. Sidman, Joyce. 2013. *What the Heart Knows: Chants, Charms & Blessings.* Houghton Mifflin Harcourt. *poems of comfort and celebration including laments, spells, invocations, promises

8. Soto, Gary. 2008. *Partly Cloudy: Poems of Love and Longing.* Houghton Mifflin Harcourt. *fresh free verse poems about love from shifting points of view of both girls and boys

9. Weatherford, Carole Boston. 2015. *Voice of Freedom: Fannie Lou Hamer: The Spirit of the Civil Rights Movement.* Candlewick. *Civil Rights information plus contemporary inspiration

10. Worth, Valerie. 1994. *All the Small Poems and Fourteen More.* Farrar, Straus & Giroux. *100+ precise and compelling free verse poems about the wonder of the ordinary

POPULAR POETRY ANTHOLOGIES

One place where we can find the work of a lot of different poets is in the classic form of the poetry anthology. Here, one or two editors gather many poems by many writers and organize them into a variety of themes or topics.

1. Carlson, Lori M. Ed. 2005. *Red Hot Salsa: Bilingual Poems on Being Young and Latino in the United States.* Henry Holt. *featuring many award-winning and contemporary Latino and Latina poets, plus teens themselves

2. Greenberg, Jan. Ed. 2001. *Heart to Heart: New Poems Inspired by Twentieth-Century American Art.* Abrams. *ekphrastic poetry with each poet writing in response to a work of art

3. Heard, Georgia. Ed. 2006 (reissued). *This Place I Know: Poems of Comfort.* Candlewick. *poets write about loss, fear, and grief

4. Hopkins, Lee Bennett. Ed. 2013. *All the World's a Stage.* Creative Editions. *poems on life's different stages, from "entrances" to "exits," with childhood, love, war, and more in between

5. Janeczko, Paul B. Ed. 2004. *Blushing: Expressions of Love.* Scholastic. *both classic and contemporary poems about new love, unrequited love, lost love, love remembered

6. Kennedy, Caroline. Ed. 2013. *Poems to Learn by Heart.* Hyperion. *100+ poems offer a wide range of options for all ages for enjoyment, memorizing, and performing

7. Lewis, J. Patrick. Ed. 2015. *National Geographic Book of Nature Poetry.* National Geographic. *vivid photographs provide a stunning background for poems about the natural world

8. Nye, Naomi Shihab. Ed. 1992. *This Same Sky: A Collection of Poems from Around the World.* Four Winds Press. *a collection of poems in English by writers from all around the world

9. Paschen, Elise and Raccah, Dominique. Eds. 2010. *Poetry Speaks: Who I Am.* Sourcebooks. *candid poems about identity, ideas, and connections in a very accessible format

10. Rampersad, Arnold and Blount, Marcellus. Eds. 2013. *Poetry for Young People: African American Poetry* (reissued, reillustrated). Sterling. *stylized illustrations accompany these powerful poems by 27 African American poets from Phillis Wheatley to contemporary poets

POPULAR NOVELS IN VERSE

Each of these books is an excellent example of a novel in verse, of how to create strong characters and dialogue, and how to experiment with a variety of poetic forms within the context of a story frame.

1. Alexander, Kwame. 2014. *The Crossover*. Houghton Mifflin Harcourt. *Twin brothers compete in basketball and love

2. Creech, Sharon. 2001. *Love That Dog*. HarperCollins. *Reluctantly, a boy comes to appreciate poetry as he writes about a beloved dog

3. Frost, Helen. 2003. *Keesha's House*. Farrar, Straus & Giroux. *seven teens' lives intersect at Keesha's uncle's safe house

4. Grimes, Nikki. 2002. *Bronx Masquerade*. Dial. *an English teacher provides an open mike opportunity where teens share and are empowered

5. McCall, Guadalupe Garcia. 2011. *Under the Mesquite*. Lee & Low. *teen girl struggles with her mother's ill health and her family's needs

6. Myers, Walter Dean. 2004. *Here in Harlem: Poems in Many Voices*. Holiday House. *the history and vibrancy of Harlem comes to life through 53 different perspectives

7. Newman, Lesléa. 2012. *October Mourning: A Song for Matthew Shepard*. Candlewick. *heartbreaking poems about the murder of Matthew Shepard from many points of view

8. Thompson, Holly. 2011. *Orchards*. Random House. *A girl spends the summer with her Japanese family while she tries to figure out her role in a classmate's suicide

9. Wolf, Allan. 2011. *The Watch That Ends the Night: Voices from the Titanic*. Candlewick. *poems illuminate the human scale of this historic voyage and its tragic end

10. Woodson, Jacqueline. 2014. *Brown Girl Dreaming*. Nancy Paulsen Books/Penguin. *Woodson tells her own life story through poems that capture personal moments as well as a slice of history

POETRY BOOKS ABOUT SPORTS

Sports and poetry may seem like an unlikely combination, but it has ancient roots with poems recited at sporting events such as victory odes at the earliest Olympics. Perhaps a poem from one of the books below can kick off an athletic competition, sporting event, or field day celebration.

1. Adoff, Arnold. 2000. *The Basket Counts*. Simon & Schuster. *distinctive free verse showcases the energy of basketball

2. Alexander, Kwame. 2016. *Booked*. Houghton Mifflin Harcourt. *Soccer is his passion, but this boy is pressured by his dad to learn vocabulary and love reading, too

3. Burg, Ann E. 2009. *All the Broken Pieces*. Scholastic. *Teen boy struggles with personal loss and prejudice while exploring his talent as a baseball pitcher in this Vietnam-era story

4. Glenn, Mel. 1997. *Jump Ball: A Basketball Season in Poems*. Lodestar Books / Dutton. *drama of high school filtered through one basketball season

5. Hopkins, Lee Bennett. Ed. 1996. *Opening Days: Sports Poems*. Harcourt. *a classic anthology featuring sports such as cycling, ice skating, skiing, tennis, karate, and weightlifting

6. Hoyte, Carol-Ann and Roemer, Heidi Bee. Eds. 2012. *And the Crowd Goes Wild!: A Global Gathering of Sports Poems*. Friesens. *a wide variety of sports played all around the world

7. Koertge, Ron. 2003. *Shakespeare Bats Cleanup*. Candlewick. *Teen boy explores poetry writing while sitting out his beloved baseball season due to illness

8. Morrison, Lillian. 2001. *Way to Go!: Sports Poems*. Wordsong/ Boyds Mills. *from track and field to swimming and surfing, all kinds of sports are captured in 42 lively poems

9. Smith, Charles R. Jr. 2003. *Hoop Queens*. Candlewick. *rap poem tributes to 12 WNBA stars

10. Smith, Charles R. Jr. 2004. *Hoop Kings*. Candlewick. *superstars of the NBA are showcased in poems and art

POETRY WEBSITES YOU NEED TO KNOW

There are many excellent websites related to poetry to explore, with information about poets, classic and contemporary poems, audio and video of poets and poems, performance suggestions, and much more. Here are a dozen of our favorite sites.

The Academy of American Poets
Poets.org

Columbia Granger's World of Poetry
ColumbiaGrangers.org

The Library of Congress Poetry and Literature Center
LOC.gov/poetry

Favorite Poem Project
FavoritePoem.org

No Water River
NoWaterRiver.com

Poetry Alive
PoetryAlive.com

Poetry Daily
Poems.com

Poetry Foundation
PoetryFoundation.org

Poetry Out Loud
PoetryOutLoud.org

Poetry Slams, Inc.
PoetrySlam.com

Poetry Speaks
PoetrySpeaks.com

Power Poetry
PowerPoetry.org

TALKING POINTS

As you read and discuss the poems in this book, the activities below can serve as "talking points" to launch or focus your discussion—and if you have your own questions, go with those!

1. **Talk about the Census demographics in your own community.** Which cultural and ethnic groups are represented? If necessary, use data available at Census.gov (use the Quick Facts link for information about your own state, city, or town).

2. **Talk about learning to drive and what a fun, important, and scary act driving is.** Do some quick research on safe driving practices. For a good source, search "Top 10 Safe Driving Tips" on HowStuffWorks.com or look for "Driving Tips for Bad Weather," particularly "Driving on Ice" at Drive-safely.net.

3. **What are your favorite after-school sports?** Poll your group about sports they have experienced, such as baseball, football, soccer, basketball, swimming, and more. Which would you like to try? Which do you enjoy most as spectator vs. participant?

4. **Talk about the experience of reading or listening to a poem (when you read it aloud) in contrast with viewing a digital video adaptation.** For example, look for the "poem movie" featuring the poem "Names" on the PFAMS blog (PFAMS.blogspot.com). Contrast what you "see" and "hear" when reading or listening to the poem with what you perceive when you watch the movie based on the poem.

5. Notice that most poems in this book do not end in a regular rhyme scheme, though some may use rhyme. **Most are examples of *free verse*.** The poem doesn't rhyme at the end of each line, but still has a structure and rhythm based on line lengths and breaks, with short lines offering greater emphasis.

6. **Sometimes poets use each of the letters of a key word to begin the lines of a poem; this is called acrostic poetry.** Highlight the first word of each line in the poem "Future Hoopsters" with American Sign Language to show how the letters of two words (*HOOPSTER HOPES*) were used, and talk about how those words echo the theme of the poem.

7. **Sometimes poets use basic graphic elements like italics, capital letters, punctuation, spacing, and indentation to add interest to their poems or to guide the reader.** Talk about how these things are used in the poems in this book. In "Tryouts" and "World Cup," the poet uses italics (to indicate the coach's lines and point of view) as well as distinctive spacing to add to the effect of each stanza.

8. Sometimes poems feature more than one main character or speaker. **Talk about how the reader or listener knows whose point of view is whose in a poem** (using quotation marks or italics as a clue) and how differences in point of view can create tension or humor. For example, in "Dracula," Lisette loves vampire movies though she covers her eyes.

9. Repetition is a key ingredient in creating some poems. Sometimes a poet uses repetition not just to enhance the sound of the poem, but to emphasize meaning. **Talk about how the poets often repeat key words or phrases.** For example, in "Locker Ness Monster," number words are repeated in different configurations to heighten the sense of confusion expressed in the poem.

10. Sometimes poets **use the element of alliteration** to repeat the same sound in the beginning of several words for greater emphasis. See if you can locate examples of alliteration (e.g., in "Black Ice" you can find w in *whirl, winter, wind*; s in *slicked, surface*; b in *black, back*; and t in *tire, treads*).

11. Sometimes poets use their imaginations to guess what it might be like if something that is not alive had a real personality. This is called **the element of personification.** Use the poems "The Waking House" or "What She Asked" to determine which words or phrases suggest that inanimate objects are living, breathing beings.

12. **Poets often use metaphors to compare one thing to another to give us a fresh perspective on both things.** See if you can identify the metaphor in the poem "First Practice," with a focus on the second stanza in particular. What two things are being compared to one another?

POETRY PERFORMANCE TIPS

It can be fun to read these poems aloud as a group using various informal theater or performance techniques.

1. **Simple props can add fun to sharing a poem** with a group or larger audience. This can be a common object mentioned in the poem as your "poetry prop," held up while reading aloud. For example, for the poem "Locker Ness Monster," hold up a locker lock before reading the poem aloud, then spin the wheel and stop at the numbers in the poem.

2. **For an atmospheric backdrop for a poem reading, project a movie still** or a movie scene related to the poem. One excellent source is IMDB.com. For example, for the poem "Dracula," project a poster for any of the Dracula films.

3. **Consider using audio sound effects or music as a backdrop for a poem reading**, where appropriate. For the poem "The Waking House," you could find short audio clips for the sounds referenced in the poem (alarm clock, blow dryer, clothes dryer, toaster, tea kettle, microwave) to play before or during the reading of the poem. One source of sounds and sound effects is SoundCloud.com.

4. Whenever a poet employs **italicized text, that can be the perfect opportunity for an interactive read aloud,** with a leader or narrator reading most of the poem, and others reading the italicized text for added emphasis.

5. When poems incorporate **number words, the names of months, or the days of the week,** that is another easy component for participation. A leader reads most of the poem, and the rest of the group or individual volunteers read the number words, months, or days for added emphasis.

6. **Whenever dialogue occurs in a poem**, a leader can read most of the poem aloud, with volunteers taking on the parts of dialogue. Take a moment to clarify whose line is whose, highlighting the text if that's helpful. Think about making a podcast recording of the reading, too.

7. **Use the American Sign Language (ASL) alphabet or signing**, if you are familiar with sign language, particularly with acrostic poems such as "Future Hoopsters." You can make the first letter of each line in ASL as you read (or another volunteer reads) the poem aloud. One source is American Sign Language University at Lifeprint.com.

8. **Invite guest readers to join you for the oral reading of a poem** to add vocal variety. For example, invite a coach to read aloud "World Cup" or "Tryouts," or record a coach reading the poem (or just the coach parts).

9. **Group reading can also be a great way to get many people involved in poetry performance.** The arrangement of lines in a poem like "Cousins," for example, lends itself to a "call and response" read-aloud in two groups: one will read the first line in the couplet stanza, and the other will read the second line in the couplet stanza.

10. With novels in verse that feature multiple characters like this one, you can easily **use readers theater as a way to perform the poems** with various volunteers acting as the characters in the book. Someone can "be" Paz, Lucesita, and Joe and read aloud all "their" poems, while a leader acts as the narrator and reads the rest.

11. **Stage a "tableau" for poems by asking volunteers to pose in scenes suggested by the poem** while a narrator reads the poem aloud. For example, choose four frozen moments from the poem "Black Ice" to create as "scenes," with one or two volunteers posing as described in the lines of the poem. Photograph and/or film the tableau and post it with the poem.

12. **Organize poetry jams**—informal gatherings especially for reading aloud poetry—to provide an opportunity for everyone to read aloud the poems they create in response to the poems in this book. Have a microphone ready, and record the readings, if possible.

ABOUT THE POETS

Biographical information, photos, and lists of some of the books by our contributing poets can be found at PomeloBooks.com. Most poets have their own websites, too, where you can find contact info for them, news about their books, and even links to their blogs. Eleven poets wrote the poems in this book that appeared first in **The Poetry Friday Anthology for Middle School**; *Janet Wong, the twelfth poet, wrote all poems in the voices of Paz, Lucesita, and Joe.*

Carmen T. Bernier-Grand
http:/www.carmenberniergrand.com
Carmen T. Bernier-Grand originally hails from Puerto Rico, but has lived in Oregon most of her life. She studied math, taught at a university in Puerto Rico, and worked as a computer programmer before writing for young people. Her books include folktales from Puerto Rico and biographies in verse: *César: ¡Sí, Se Puede! Yes, We can!*; *Frida: ¡Viva la vida! Long Live Life!*; and *Diego: Bigger Than Life.*

Robyn Hood Black
http://www.robynhoodblack.com
Robyn Hood Black grew up in Orlando, Florida, and was the editor of her elementary school newspaper. She taught middle school English and now speaks about writing and art in school assemblies and workshops, conferences, and festivals across the country. She is the author of *Sir Mike*, a rhyming reader, and *Wolves*, a nonfiction book, and her poems have appeared in several anthologies, magazines, and journals. She also creates "literary art with a vintage vibe" through her business, artsyletters (http://artsyletters.com).

Joseph Bruchac
http://josephbruchac.com
Joseph Bruchac has been writing poetry, short stories, novels, anthologies, professional resources, and music reflecting his Abenaki Indian heritage and Native American traditions for over three decades. He has authored more than 120 books for children and adults, including these poetry collections: *Thirteen Moons on Turtle's Back: A Native American Year of Moons*, *The Earth Under Sky Bear's Feet: Native American Poems of the Land*, *Between Earth and Sky: Legends of Native American Sacred Places*, *Four Ancestors: Stories, Songs, and Poems from Native North America*, and *The Circle of Thanks.*

Jen Bryant

http://www.jenbryant.com

Jen Bryant's childhood was filled with opera, music, and horses in Flemington, Pennsylvania. As an adult, she taught school for several years and then began her writing career with nonfiction books for young readers. Her biographies for young people—*A River of Words, A Splash of Red,* and *The Right Word*—have garnered many awards and distinctions. And her novels in verse have been recognized as spare, remarkable, and empathetic, including *The Trial, Pieces of Georgia, Ringside, 1925: Views from the Scopes Trial,* and *Kaleidoscope Eyes.* She keeps a regular blog (http://www.jenbryant.com/blog/) and newsletter, too.

Margarita Engle

http://margaritaengle.com

Margarita Engle's life experiences are tied to both California and Cuba, and these settings feature prominently in many of her historical novels in verse. She received a Newbery honor for *The Surrender Tree* and has garnered many other awards for her work, including the Pura Belpré Medal, Américas Award, Jane Addams Award, and most recently the PEN Literary Award, among others. She studied agronomy and botany and worked in these fields professionally before writing for young people full-time. In her spare time, she also enjoys helping her husband with training wilderness search and rescue dogs. Her many novels in verse include:

- *The Poet Slave of Cuba*
- *The Surrender Tree*
- *Tropical Secrets: Holocaust Refugees in Cuba*
- *The Firefly Letters: A Suffragette's Journey to Cuba*
- *Hurricane Dancers: The First Caribbean Pirate Shipwreck*
- *The Wild Book*
- *Mountain Dog*
- *The Lightning Dreamer*
- *Silver People: Voices from the Panama Canal*
- *Lion Island*

Charles Ghigna
http://charlesghigna.com
Charles Ghigna, also known as "Father Goose®," lives in Alabama and is the author of more than 5,000 poems and 100 books, including many picture books, easy readers, concept books, and poetry collections such as *Riddle Rhymes, Animal Poems, Animal Trunk, Tickle Day, Score! 50 Poems to Motivate and Inspire, Christmas Is Coming,* and *A Fury of Motion: Poems for Boys.* He is a frequent presenter, poetry editor, and columnist.

Avis Harley
https://www.poetryfoundation.org/poems-and-poets/poets/detail/avis-harley
Avis Harley grew up in British Columbia, Canada, and has spent most of her career in the field of education. She conducts workshops and mentors young poets. Her poetry is characterized by its diversity and experimentation. She enjoys trying poetry in all its different formats and is adept at demonstrating poetic form for children. Her work includes:
- *Fly with Poetry: An ABC of Poetry*
- *Leap into Poetry: More ABCs of Poetry*
- *Sea Stars: Saltwater Poems*
- *The Monarch's Progress: Poems with Wings*
- *African Acrostics: A Word in Edgeways*

Julie Larios
http://julielarios.blogspot.com
Julie Larios lives in Seattle, Washington, and taught for many years on the faculty of the Vermont College of Fine Arts in their MFA-Writing for Children program. She is the winner of a Pushcart Prize and has received recognitions and fellowships for her poetry for adults, as well as for children. Her work appears in many anthologies and includes the poetry picture books *Yellow Elephant: A Bright Bestiary, Imaginary Menagerie: A Book of Curious Creatures,* and *Have You Ever Done That?* Her blog, The Drift Record (http://julielarios.blogspot.com), features regular, insightful entries on savoring, writing, and teaching poetry.

Amy Ludwig VanDerwater

http://www.amyludwigvanderwater.com

Amy Ludwig VanDerwater's work has appeared in multiple anthologies and she is a frequent and popular workshop presenter and literacy consultant. She is a former fifth grade teacher and her current blogs on poetry and writing, *Poem Farm* (*PoemFarm.AmyLV.com*) and *Sharing Our Notebooks* (http://www.sharingournotebooks.amylv.com), are both highly regarded resources on the writing and teaching of poetry. Her poetry and picture books for children include *Forest Has a Song*, *Every Day Birds*, and the forthcoming *Read! Read! Read!*, *Dreaming of You, With My Hands: Poems About Making Things*, and a professional resource book, *Poems Are Teachers: Learning Craft Line By Line*.

Virginia Euwer Wolff

http://www.virginiaeuwerwolff.com

Virginia Euwer Wolff hails from Portland, Oregon, where she grew up in a log house with no electricity, but many, many books. She taught elementary school and later high school English and published the award-winning "*Make Lemonade* trilogy" (*Make Lemonade, True Believer,* and *This Full House*), ground-breaking novels in verse. She now lives on the east coast where she is an accomplished violinist and avid gardener.

Janet Wong

http://www.janetwong.com

Janet Wong was born in Los Angeles, the daughter of a Chinese father and Korean mother. She earned her law degree at Yale and practiced corporate and labor law, but was unhappy and turned to writing for young people. She studied under poetry mentor Myra Cohn Livingston, who helped her publish her first collection of poetry *Good Luck Gold*, and has been a dynamo ever since. Her poetry includes the verse novels *Minn and Jake* and *Minn and Jake's Almost Terrible Summer,* plus these works and more:

- *Good Luck Gold and Other Poems*
- *A Suitcase of Seaweed and Other Poems*
- *Behind the Wheel: Poems about Driving*
- *Knock on Wood: Poems about Superstitions*
- *Twist: Yoga Poems*

POEM CREDITS

For permission to reprint any of the poems in this book, please contact Pomelo Books or the individual poets listed here (directly or through their agents). Each poem listed here has all rights reserved. If you need help getting in touch with a poet, just let us know and we'll be happy to connect you.

If it doesn't feel right to copy it . . . please *don't!*

Carmen T. Bernier-Grand: "Dracula"; copyright ©2013 by Carmen T. Bernier-Grand. Used with permission of the author.

Robyn Hood Black: "Locker Ness Monster"; copyright ©2013 by Robyn Hood Black. Used with permission of the author.

Jen Bryant: "Tryouts" and "World Cup"; copyright ©2013 by Jen Bryant. Used with permission of the author.

Joseph Bruchac: "Black Ice"; copyright ©2013 by Joseph Bruchac. Used with permission of the author.

Margarita Engle: "Who Am I?"; copyright ©2013 by Margarita Engle. Used with permission of the author.

Charles Ghigna: "The Waking House"; copyright ©2013 by Charles Ghigna. Used with permission of the author.

Avis Harley: "Future Hoopsters"; copyright ©2013 by Avis Harley. Used with permission of the author.

Julie Larios: "Names"; copyright ©2013 by Julie Larios. Used with permission of the author.

Amy Ludwig VanDerwater: "First Practice"; copyright ©2013 by Amy Ludwig VanDerwater. Used with permission of Curtis Brown, Ltd.

Charles Waters: "Cousins"; copyright ©2013 by Charles Waters. Used with permission of the author.

Virginia Euwer Wolff: "What She Asked"; copyright ©2013 by Virginia Euwer Wolff. Used with permission of Curtis Brown, Ltd.

Janet Wong: poems with the headings "Paz," "Lucesita," and "Joe"; copyright ©2016 by Janet S. Wong. Used with permission of the author.

POET INDEX

TITLE INDEX

ABOUT VARDELL AND WONG

Sylvia M. Vardell is Professor at Texas Woman's University and teaches courses in children's and young adult literature. She has published five books on literature, as well as over 25 book chapters and 100 journal articles. Her current work focuses on poetry for young people, including a regular blog, PoetryforChildren.blogspot.com, since 2006. Her favorite team experience was being part of the Mermaids Drill Team in middle school. No mermaid tail, but lots of cheering, dancing, and good times with friends.

Janet S. Wong is a graduate of Yale Law School and a former lawyer who became a children's poet. Her work has been featured on *The Oprah Winfrey Show* and other shows. She is the author of 30 books for children and teens on chess, creative recycling, yoga, superstitions, driving, and more. Always a slow runner and a below-average athlete, she grew up wishing she could be on a sports team—but settled for the debate team instead, where she could have used more of Lucesita's flair for the dramatic.

Together, Vardell and Wong are the creative forces behind *The Poetry Friday Anthology* series.

ABOUT THE POETRY FRIDAY ANTHOLOGY® SERIES

In *The Poetry Friday Anthology* series, we have created a unique resource that blends original poetry by today's best and brightest poets writing for young people and teaching strategies that make it easy to introduce poetry, engage readers, and reinforce learning objectives. The organizational features of each book make it quick and easy to find, share, and teach poetry at multiple levels and across the curriculum. We strive to balance communicating the joy and playfulness of poetry with learning important concepts and skills.

THE POETRY FRIDAY ANTHOLOGY FOR MIDDLE SCHOOL

110 poems by 71 poets about new schools, coping with family, playing soccer, and texting friends, with *Take 5!* mini-lessons for every poem *(an NCTE Poetry Notable)*

THE POETRY FRIDAY ANTHOLOGY FOR K-5

218 poems by 76 poets about school, pets, favorite sports, food, friends, free time, vacation, books, and more, with *Take 5!* mini-lessons for each poem

THE POETRY OF SCIENCE

248 science poems on a wide variety of topics, including engineering, technology, and inventions *(an NSTA Recommends companion book)*

THE POETRY FRIDAY ANTHOLOGY FOR CELEBRATIONS

156 poems by 115 poets in English and Spanish about celebrations from Halloween to National Pizza Week to National Bike Month and more *(an ILA-CL/R Notable Book for a Global Society)*

For more information about *The Poetry Friday Anthology* series, please visit **PomeloBooks.com**.

"I didn't think it was my job
to accept what everyone said I was
and who I should be."

—Benjamin Alire Sáenz

YOUR OWN
PERSONAL POWER PAGES

DOODLE SKETCH DRAW LIST WRITE
BRAINSTORM HEARTSTORM

YOUR OWN
PERSONAL POWER PAGES

YOUR OWN
PERSONAL POWER PAGES

DOODLE   SKETCH   DRAW   LIST   WRITE
BRAINSTORM   HEARTSTORM